to teachers and parents

This is a LADYBIRD LEADER book, one of a series specially produced to meet the very real need for carefully planned *first information books* that instantly attract enquiring minds and stimulate reluctant readers.

The subject matter and vocabulary have been selected with expert assistance, and the brief and simple text is printed in large, clear type.

Children's questions are anticipated and facts presented in a logical sequence. Where possible, the books show what happened in the past and what is relevant today.

Special artwork has been commissioned to set a standard rarely seen in books for this reading age and at this price.

Full colour illustrations are on all 48 pages to give maximum impact and provide the extra enrichment that is the aim of all Ladybird Leaders.

Acknowledgments

The illustration on page 32 is by John Leigh-Pemberton, and the photograph of Adelie Penguins in the Antarctic, on the front endpaper, is by Popperfoto.

A Ladybird Leader

polar
regions

by P H Armstrong B Sc M A Ph D

with illustrations by Gerald Witcomb M S I A D

Ladybird Books Ltd Loughborough 1977

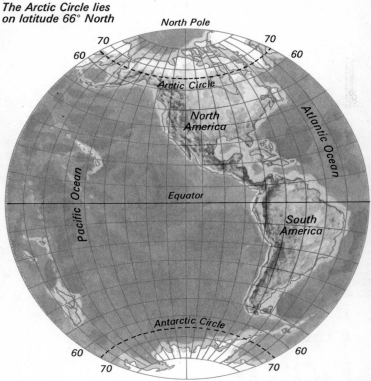

The Arctic Circle lies on latitude 66° North

North Pole

70 70

60 60

Arctic Circle

North America

Atlantic Ocean

Pacific Ocean

Equator

South America

Antarctic Circle

60 60

70 70

South Pole

The Antarctic Circle lies on latitude 66° South

Polar regions

The part of the world
around the North Pole
is called the Arctic.

The part around the South Pole
is called the Antarctic.

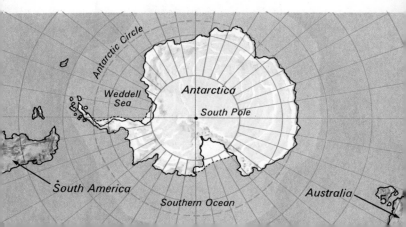

The Arctic is an ocean
with land most of the way round it,
but the Antarctic
is a mass of land
with sea all the way round it.

Weather

In both the Arctic and Antarctic
the sun's rays give
very little heat,
and it is very very cold
for much of the time.

In the Antarctic the temperature
is sometimes as low as −85°C.
It often snows.
Winds are sometimes very strong.
Strong icy winds
that blow the snow about
are called *blizzards*.

Survival

Life in polar regions
can be very hard.

Crops cannot grow
and so most food has to be brought
from elsewhere.

There is danger of *frost-bite*
(the freezing of fingers, toes,
or parts of the face)
because of the cold and icy wind.

The glare of the sun on the snow
can cause blindness.
Very thick warm clothes
and special goggles are worn.

Land of the midnight sun

Close to the North and South Poles
it is daylight
for several months each year.
In summer the sun never sets
and can be seen at midnight.

1 am   6 am   12 noon   6 pm   midnight

Land of permanent darkness

In winter it stays dark
for months on end.

The northern and southern lights

At night, close to the North
and South Poles,
parts of the sky glow pink,
green or yellow.

These lights may move across the sky
and flicker.

They are very beautiful.
Sometimes the northern lights
are called the *aurora borealis*
and the southern lights
the *aurora australis.*

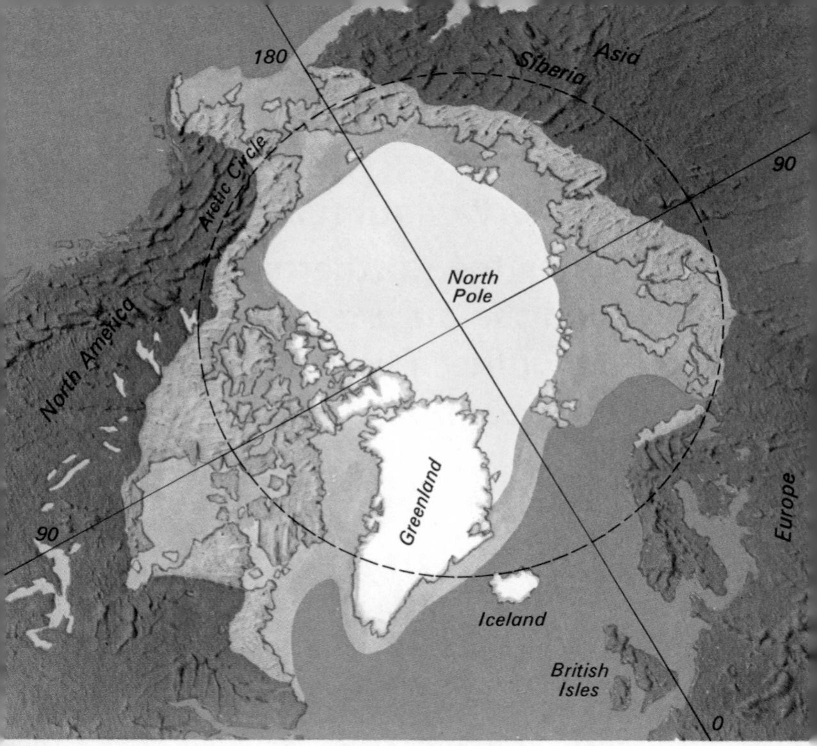
180
Asia
Siberia
90
Arctic Circle
North America
North Pole
Greenland
90
Europe
Iceland
British Isles
0

Ice caps
Sea always frozen
Sea seasonally open
Tundra frozen
Land unfrozen
Sea open

Ice-sheets

On land in the Antarctic and in parts of the Arctic more snow falls in winter than melts in summer.

As layer piles on layer
the air is squeezed out
and ice forms.

In Greenland and the Antarctic
there are ice-sheets
thousands of metres thick.

Deep cracks or *crevasses*
sometimes form in the ice.

These can be very dangerous
to people crossing the ice.

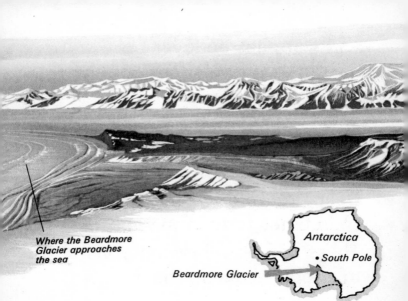

Where the Beardmore
Glacier approaches
the sea

Antarctica

• South Pole

Beardmore Glacier

Glaciers and icebergs

A *glacier* is a mass of ice
slowly moving downhill.

Where the glacier meets the sea
icebergs break off and float away.

In an iceberg much more ice
is below the water
than shows above it.

Icebergs are very dangerous
to ships.
Some ships have sunk
after hitting an iceberg
at night or in fog.

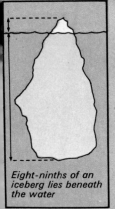

Eight-ninths of an
iceberg lies beneath
the water

Sea-ice and ice-floes

When it is very cold
the sea freezes.

Sometimes the sea-ice is fixed
to the land,
but rafts of *pack-ice* drift across
the polar seas.

In winter large areas of the sea
are frozen
and ships cannot get through.

Overland travel

On one Antarctic expedition
in 1908 - 1909,
men on foot pulled sledges
2600 kilometres in 120 days.

Ponies have been used
to pull sledges
in both the Arctic and Antarctic.

Skis are useful
for short journeys.

Dogs

Husky dogs are used
to pull sledges
in the Arctic and Antarctic.

They weigh 25 - 45 kilograms
and have thick hair
8 - 15 centimetres long
to keep them warm.

Husky dogs are very strong:
a team of nine dogs can pull
a load of half a tonne
40 - 50 kilometres a day
for many days.

With a light load they can travel
over 150 kilometres in a day.

Vehicles

Tractors are now used
on many polar expeditions.

The *Sno-cat* can carry
a load of nearly three tonnes
and can tow another six tonnes.

It can cross hard or soft snow.

For small groups of men
a motor-toboggan which can pull
about a tonne
is sometimes most useful.

Ice-breakers

These are ships that are used
to cut a way through the ice
so that other ships may pass.

They have very strong hulls
and big engines.

An ice-breaker has a sloping bow
to let the ship ride up over the ice
and smash it.

Aircraft

Some air routes now pass
over the Arctic.

Helicopters are used
in both the Arctic and Antarctic
to take scientists
to places where they work.

In Canada aircraft are fitted
with skis and land on frozen lakes
in winter.

The Tundra

Many areas in the Arctic
are free from snow
for only a few months in summer.
Lichens, mosses, grasses,
and bushes up to one metre high
grow in these *tundra* areas.

Arctic Poppies

In spring the tundra is a mass
of flowers.

All the plants flower together
so that they can set seeds
before the cold weather returns.

Arctic animals

Some mammals and birds
that live in the Arctic
are white all the time.

Polar bears live in places
where there is almost always
some snow.

They are white all the time
so that they can creep
towards their prey unseen.

Rock Ptarmigan

Summer plumage

Winter plumage

Birds such as the ptarmigan
and mammals such as
the Arctic fox
have brown feathers or fur
in summer
and become white in the winter.

Arctic Fox

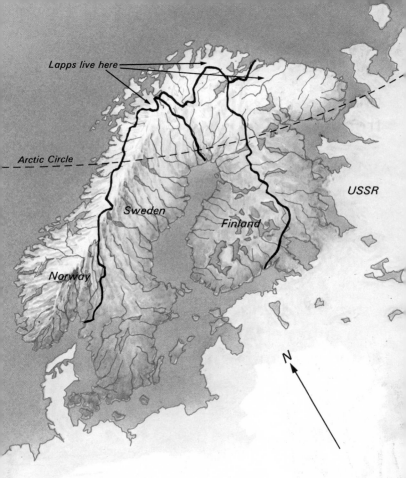

Lapps live here

Arctic Circle

Sweden

Finland

USSR

Norway

N

The Lapps

The Lapps live in northern Sweden, Norway, Finland and Russia.

They follow the herds of reindeer.
They eat reindeer meat
and make things
from the bones and skins.

The Eskimos

These people live in Greenland,
Alaska, and Arctic Canada.

They live by hunting seals
and fishing.

They make almost all they need
from bone, stone, skins
and driftwood.

Eskimos make skin canoes
called *kayaks*
and in some parts of Canada
build snow-houses or *igloos.*

Today many Eskimos live in houses:
some work as guides
for visiting hunters,
and others sell carvings.

Nansen

In 1893 the Arctic explorer Nansen
took his ship, the *Fram,*
into the Arctic ice,
where it was frozen in.

He wanted to prove
that ice drifted slowly
across the Arctic Ocean.

Ice

Arctic Circle

1893

North Pole

1896

Nansen

N

The *Fram* came out of the ice
on the other side of the ocean
in 1896.

Reaching the North Pole

The first man to reach the North Pole
was Admiral Peary in 1909.

Another American, Byrd,
was the first to fly over the Pole
in an aeroplane.
He flew from Spitzbergen in 1926.

Admiral Richard Byrd

Antarctic exploration

The first men to reach the South Pole were led by the Norwegian explorer Roald Amundsen in 1911.

He reached the Pole a month before Captain Robert Scott's British party.

Amundsen's sledges were pulled by dogs.

Roald Amundsen

Captain Robert Scott

Scott's men pulled their own sledges
on foot: they travelled
much more slowly and died
on the way home.

The Commonwealth Trans-Antarctic expedition

The next men to reach
the South Pole overland
were the members
of a British-New Zealand expedition
in 1958.

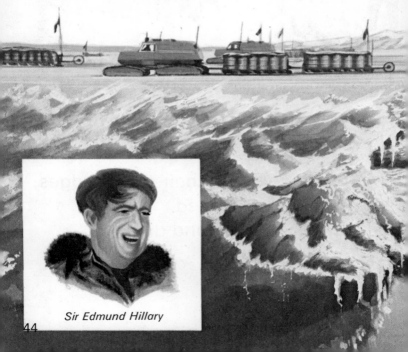

Sir Edmund Hillary

They were led
by Sir Vivian Fuchs
and Sir Edmund Hillary.

Sno-cats were used
and the 3500 kilometres
took 99 days.

Sir Vivian Fuchs

Antarctica

The Antarctic land mass
is called *Antarctica.*

It is almost all covered with ice.

There are very few plants
and no large land animals.

No one lives in the Antarctic
except for a few scientists
who stay there for a year or two
at a time.

Today scientists from many countries
work in the Antarctic.

They study the weather, the rocks,
the ice and the life in the seas.

The scientist in the picture
will check the signals
from this balloon
to see how strong the wind is
far above the ground.

Scientist releasing a radio sonde balloon

The Antarctic seas

The Antarctic seas are full of life.

The many tiny plants and animals
are eaten by fish.

The fish are eaten by penguins.

Penguins are birds that have wings
like flippers.

They cannot fly but can swim
very well.

Sometimes many thousands
of pairs of penguins
nest together in 'rookeries'.

*Penguins in
the Antarctic*

Leopard Seal

Seals

Seals are mammals
that live in the sea.

Like penguins, they cannot
move well on land.

There are ten kinds of seals
in the Antarctic seas.

The leopard seal feeds mainly
on penguins.

A large bull elephant seal
weighs three tonnes.

Some seals used to be hunted
for their fur.

Whaling

Whales, like seals, are mammals
that live in the sea,
but whales have no legs
and so can never come onto land.

The whales that live in the seas
round Antarctica
are caught for the oil
they have in their bodies.

Some people say
too many whales are being killed
and one day there will be none left.

Hump-backed Whale

Conservation

Many countries have now agreed
that the animals of Antarctica
and the Antarctic seas
are to be specially protected
and studied.

These marked penguins may be
seen again elsewhere.

Scientists will know how far
they have travelled.

Index